Reiki

A Complete Guide to Reiki Energy Healing

Jamie Parr

Table of Contents

Introduction 1

Chapter 1: What Is Reiki? 2

Chapter 2: Reiki and Its History 11

Chapter 3: Becoming a Reiki Practitioner 21

Chapter 4: Reiki's Healing Magic 30

Chapter 5: Reiki Self-Help – Can It Be Done? 40

Chapter 6: Using Reiki on Others 50

Conclusion 59

Introduction

Congratulations on choosing this book and thank you for doing so!

Reiki is not something that you can easily explain, but rather, it something that you *feel*. Those who have never explored the more spiritual side of life might have difficulty being open to the idea that such a method of healing could exist. But it does, and not only does it exist, it is an incredible healing practice like no other.

This book aims to serve as an introductory guide to Reiki and details the history of Reiki, and the belief system surrounding it. You will also soon learn about the different ways Reiki can be used, as well as the steps required to become a qualified Reiki practitioner.

While Reiki has a variety of uses, it should be noted that it should never be used to entirely replace modern medicine, particularly when dealing with a serious illness. Rather, Reiki works in conjunction with modern medical treatments, helping you to heal in a more holistic fashion.

Thank you once again for taking the time to read this book. I hope you find it to be both interesting, and informative.

Chapter 1: What Is Reiki?

Many cultures believe that true healing begins from within with the mind, body, and soul. Reiki is a Japanese energy healing therapy that has taken the world by storm in recent years. It is a healing practice where the *Master* or *Healer* attempts to facilitate the transfer of positive energy by placing their hands on or over different parts of the body. The aim of the practice is to remove negative energy by transferring it out of your body, and replacing it with positive, healing energy.

The Origins of Reiki

The word *Reiki* comes from a combination of two Japanese words. The first word is *Rei,* which means "God's wisdom" or "higher power." The second word is *Ki,* which means "life force energy." is a Japanese practice which first emerged somewhere in the late 1800s. Practitioners believe that the healing powers of this practice come from the universal transfer of power, which the practitioner transfers to their patient. Reiki advocates believe that this practice works by manipulating the energy fields that surround our bodies. Its healing benefits have caused Reiki's popularity to soar over the years, and approximately 1.2-million American adults participated in some form of Reiki therapy or similar at least once in the past year. A 2014 report in The Washington Post revealed that more than 60 hospitals supposedly offered Reiki healing as part of their services for patients who wanted it.

Reiki involves stress reduction techniques that rely on the use of the hands to conduct the healing process. The energies that flow around the outside of our bodies are referred to as *auras*. An *aura* is described as the human energy field, and some believe that this energy field comes in different colors that emanate around a person. Sometimes not just a person, but it could also be present around an animal or even an inanimate object, for that matter. Not everyone has the ability to see *auras* just like that on their own. Usually, it is psychics who claim to have that gift, and they are able to go as far as seeing the size, color, and the vibration intensity that is generated by a person's *aura*. This ethereal radiation surrounds each living being and it usually surrounds them within the space of two or three feet of the body. Most people are consumed by only believing and seeing what is directly in front of them, and oftentimes they forget there is a whole other spiritual world out there that they are completely overlooking. Your aura is directly affected by the positive and negative thoughts that you have. Therefore, any negative thought or bias will affect your wellbeing, whether you do it consciously or otherwise. When your energy levels diminish, your body and its organs eventually pay the price. Reiki works with this energy field to remove the negative energies, and replace them with positive, healing ones.

The Energy Around Us

The practice of Reiki is based on the idea that our health comes from the *Ki* that flows through our bodies. This *Ki* is the energy that is believed to flow through us and all around us. Reiki advocates believe that *Ki* is the one responsible for the healthy organs in our system. When the flow of *Ki* is adversely disrupted in any way, it will affect your body and cause it illness. Helping the *Ki* flow freely means that positive energy is able to move freely throughout your body, thus promoting good health and an overall happy mind and body.

When this energy life force within us is high, we feel alive and a lot more energetic. We walk with a bounce in our step and a renewed zest for life. No problem seems too difficult to overcome with this happier, more positive outlook on life. When our energy levels are low, however, we feel sick, lethargic, fatigued, miserable, and like the whole world is out to get us.

The Western world is slowly beginning to realize the incredible power of the mind and body connection. Reiki advocates believe that by manipulating the energy fields that surround our body, we can dramatically change the way we feel. You see, our bodies are an incredible thing. They work hard to keep us alive every day, regulating all the bodily functions needed to keep us strong and healthy. From our organ functions, all the way to our emotions, the human body is nature's most incredible machine. A mighty force of energy exists in your body, helping it to maintain its balance and harmony. While this is a force that you may not be able to see with your naked eye, this *Ki* is extremely powerful and vital to your health and wellbeing.

The Mind-Body Connection

There's a lot more to Reiki than meets the eye. It seems to be a simple enough concept, but often many are surprised by just how great of an impact this healing modality can have.

Anyone can learn about the energy points in their bodies, but achieving a deep, meaningful connection is something that is going to require commitment, persistence, perseverance, and lots of practice. It can take quite some time to become proficient at working with the body's energy points to perform a Reiki healing.

Your body's mass of energy is always moving and ever-changing. The energy that is both within and around you is also constantly changing. Every time that you move, think, digest your food, breathe, and even when you rest or while you sleep, your body's energy is constantly flowing through your nervous system. The nervous system coordinates both your involuntary and voluntary actions, transmitting signals from your various body parts to the brain. When you move your arm, that's your nervous system at work voluntarily. When you digest that big meal you've just had, that's your nervous system involuntarily working.

Reiki works by ensuring that the energy flowing through your body and nervous system does so without hinderance. Reiki is one of the best natural ways of healing the body, mind, and soul. It is safe to be practiced on all ages, young and old alike.

The Reiki practice is simple enough that with time, anyone can learn Reiki for self-healing, and this book will serve as a great introduction to doing so. The very best way to learn and experience Reiki for yourself, however, is by training in-person with a master practitioner. Upon completing this book, you may decide that seeking in-person training from a Reiki master is something you would like to pursue.

Reiki's Close Relatives

Reiki has close ties with another similar practice that also focuses on energy healing. This practice is often referred to as *'Chakra healing'*. Originating from the Sanskrit word for "wheel," chakras have long been hailed as the essence of life, the "spinning, colored wheels" of energy in your bodies that awaken every cell in your being. The first depictions of chakras came from the Hindu Scriptures known as The Vedas, and they date back thousands of years. According to these scriptures, chakras control the energy that flows in the human body, and are responsible for keeping us vibrant and healthy, both physically and mentally. Some believe that there are 114 chakras in total, though only seven are considered the main chakras of life.

Each of these seven chakras is connected to the body's major organs. Since your body is constantly on the move, working even when you sleep, it is important that the seven chakras remain as open, fluid, and aligned as possible so there are no energy blocks that will eventually compromise your health. If you were to picture your body like a pipe, imagine what would happen if that pipe had bends and curves along the way instead of being straight and smooth like it is supposed to be. Those bends and curves become obstacles, preventing your energy from fluidly sailing through.

Chakra healing is not the only Eastern practice that advocates moving and unblocking your energy centers. From a more religious and spiritual standpoint, energy movements are the fundamental core practice which many traditions have been based upon. Ancient religions have long understood that energy is an essential element of our existence. Qigong, Reiki, Yoga, Chakra Healing, and Tai Chi are prime examples of the ancient practice that focus on manipulating energy for the purpose of helping our bodies achieve better harmony, health, and wellbeing.

It Is Not a Religion

Although religion does have spiritual components to it, Reiki is *not a religion*. You are not required to believe in anything specific. It is merely a simple practice that focuses on all-natural healing without reliance on modern medicine.

Why Heal the Body's Energy?

The spiritual side of life is something that must be honored and respected. Unfortunately, in today's busy world, this also happens to be a side of life that gets neglected too often. Reiki healing is all about embracing your spirituality as a part of who you are.

Pain relief, stress, chronic anxiety, depression, and a number of other health conditions can be improved with regular Reiki practice. **Additionally,** Reiki can be immensely beneficial for both the practitioner and the client. It can bring about a feeling of peace and harmony for both parties by dissolving the energy blocks you both possess, allowing the natural healing process to begin. The human body is an incredible thing. If given the chance, the body will always try to heal itself and Reiki is meant to encourage that process.

Reiki is capable of healing various conditions, and avid practitioners believe that it is a complete therapy on its own, although it is common these days to pair Reiki as a complementary treatment to enhance its effectiveness. Here are some of the benefits you stand to gain from Reiki:

- Clears the mind and improves focus and concentration. Greater clarity of mind will make life's challenges seem a lot easier to handle.

- Promotes natural healing within the body. Reiki supports the immune system and allows the body to rid itself of harmful toxins.

- Encourages spiritual growth and cleanses your emotional state. It heals the mind to bring about peace and calm. Reiki advocates believe that once the mind is healed, the body can begin to heal itself. The many maladies of the body are often exacerbated by the mental and emotional state that we are in.

- Releasing the negativity in your life becomes easier. In doing so, it will feel like a heavy weight has been lifted off your shoulders.

- It helps to minimize the symptoms of depression and anxiety.

- It can be used to treat a range of illnesses from the common cold and flu to serious medical conditions.

- Other ailments Reiki has been known to cure include skin problems, headaches, sore throat, fatigue, insomnia, impotence, stress, lack of confidence, bruises, and cuts.

Once you have become a Reiki healer, it is possible to heal yourself without having to rely on anyone else. You can practice it when and where you want. Although it is not recommended to forego regular treatments for serious medical conditions, Reiki can be very beneficial when used alongside Western medicine.

Chapter 2: Reiki and Its History

It all started with a man named *Mikao Usui* (18 August 1865 - 9 March 1926). Usui was born in the small village of *Tanai, Japan*. His family were the descendants of a famous samurai clan. On his memorial stone, it is mentioned that Usui's family origins can be traced back to the *Chiba clan*. As a young man, Usui would travel and study extensively. Sometime in his 50s, it is believed that Usui went through a difficult period in his life. He grew apart from his wife and two children. Most of his life remains a mystery, but what most people agree on is that Usui discovered Reiki in 1920 when he was 55 years old.

Like many cultures during that time, the Japanese relied on word-of-mouth to pass down their stories and their customs from one generation to the next. Unfortunately, this led to a lot of the wisdom and knowledge being lost or watered down. Although credited as the founder of Reiki, there are many who believe that the healing techniques used in this practice were actually first used by Buddha. Others claim this type of healing goes as far back as the ancient civilizations of *Mu* and *Atlantis*. Of course, without concrete proof, we can only speculate how Reiki originated. What we can be certain of is that it was at the very least *rediscovered* by Usui. Usui came from a family that spent eleven generations practicing Buddhism. After he finished his studies in school, Usui went on to study allopathic medicine. Usui became sick when a cholera epidemic spread through Tokyo. During his hospitalization, the story goes that he had a spiritual experience. This experience inspired him to study the teachings of his ancestors in greater detail. He joined a Zen monastery and began studying the ancient *Sanskrit* and *Sutras*. After many years of studying, Usui stumbled upon a reference to an ancient form of healing. As he dived deeper into the subject, he discovered methods, formulas, and symbols that detailed how to practice and master the art of healing using your hands. Usui now had the technical knowledge to practice this healing technique. What he was lacking now was the knowledge to turn those teachings into reality.

He realized that he needed to find out how to turn on and activate this healing power. He finally decided to seek out the final piece of the puzzle through meditation and set out on a quest to Mount Kurama.

His Time on Mount Kurama

For his personal quest, Usui had to request leave from the monastery. When he reached the top of the mountain, he picked up twenty-one pebbles. He then took the pebbles and placed them in front of himself. Usui then sat down and prepared to begin his meditation. With each day that passed, he would throw away one pebble to mark the day. Throughout the twenty-one days, Usui fasted, prayed, meditated, and read the sutras. On the final day of his fast, he prayed to God and asked that he be shown the light. Suddenly, there was a burst of bright light in the sky that started heading rapidly towards him. It hit him directly on his forehead where the third-eye chakra is located, knocking him unconscious. While in this state, Usui saw a vision of the same symbols he had read about earlier in the sutras. This was the confirmation that he knew he needed. He knew that he had found the missing piece of the puzzle.

Once Usui had regained consciousness, he traveled down from the mountain, now equipped with knowledge and Reiki techniques. During his journey down the mountain, he stubbed his toe. As he cupped it with his hands, he noticed that the pain subsided. He immediately rushed into a restaurant in the nearby village where there was a waitress who was complaining about a bad toothache. Usui offered to place his hands on her cheek and miraculously, her pain vanished. After he had some rest, Usui made his way back to the monastery. Upon his arrival, he found his friend in bed suffering from arthritic pain. Once more, Usui helped to alleviate the pain. He called this healing gift from God *'Reiki'*. Usui decided to develop a system that would allow him to pass on his knowledge and open this channel of healing to all who were eager to learn.

The experiences that Usui went through became known as the *Four Miracles:*

- Being hit in the third eye chakra by a blinding white light.

- Finally discovering the final piece of the puzzle to his quest.

- Healing himself.

- Healing the waitress and his friend at the monastery.

Over the next several years, Usui trained 2,000 students. Out of these students, nineteen would become Reiki masters themselves. He would even take his knowledge to the slums of Kyoto where he could work on healing the beggars. Usui was reminded during this time that it was not enough to focus on healing the body alone. He realized that it was equally important to heal the human spirit and the mind. The rest of his life was spent honing and developing his Reiki wisdom and techniques, teaching and passing on everything that he knew. Since Usui's students were a mix of traditional Japanese and Western allopathic believers, he knew that he had to develop a method that could easily be accepted across any religion or culture.

Thus, Usui fashioned Reiki to have no dogma or religious beliefs attached to the practice. This meant that Reiki was a universal practice that could be accepted by anyone who was willing to embrace what the healing practice was all about. His work developing Reiki was honored by the Japanese emperor named Tenno, who awarded Usui with a doctorate degree.

The Great Kanto Earthquake

In 1923, the Great Kanto earthquake devastated the city of Tokyo. Usui and his students assembled themselves around those who were injured in the catastrophe, using Reiki to heal them as best they could.

Leaving a Legacy

Six years after he founded Reiki, Usui passed away. Before he did, Usui chose Dr. Chujiro Hayashi as the next Reiki grandmaster. Usui was cremated and his ashes were placed in the Tokyo Zen monastery. Upon his death, Hayashi immediately assumed the responsibilities of the Grand Master. Hayashi would go on to train another sixteen reiki masters under his tutelage. Hayashi would also create a set formula that he used in his training.

The Life of Dr. Chujiro Hayashi

Hayashi was born in Japan to an upper-middle-class family. He was a qualified physician and a retired marine commander. Hayashi went on to set up a clinic near the palace of the emperor in Tokyo. Each day, Hayashi's students would hold healing sessions at the clinic. If there were those who couldn't leave their homes or travel, the students would go to them. During his time as the second grandmaster, Hayashi would write many reports on the method he developed to treat various ailments. His treatments also incorporated the use of special diets to help the healing process.

The discovery of whole-body treatment was perhaps Hayashi's greatest discovery. He realized that the universal life force could travel to any part of the body where healing was required. Hayashi noted that a whole-body healing process was necessary to cure any emotional or physical blocks. During his practice, Hayashi would treat all sorts of people, including the well-connected and the wealthy. His wife would continue to run the clinic after Hayashi passed away.

Hayashi trained many students when he was the grandmaster, and many of his teachings are still influential in Reiki today.

Madam Hawayo Takata

Madam Takata became the third Reiki grandmaster after Hayashi. When she was seventeen years old, she married Seiichi Takata and they had a very happy marriage. Tragically, her husband passed away after thirteen years of marriage. Madam Takata was left to raise their two children on her own. The stress and pressure of the entire ordeal had adverse effects on her health. Within five years of her husband passing away, doctors diagnosed Madam Takata with nervous exhaustion. Her health became so bad that she reached a point where she needed surgery. She was also suffering from respiratory problems at the time, which meant that using anesthetic during the surgery could potentially kill her.

Madam Takata was going through a very depressing and trying time in her life. Yet, even though she had already been through so much, Madam Takata had to undergo even more pain when her sister tragically died. With her parents back in Tokyo, it was Madam Takata's traditional responsibility to bring the news of her sister's death in person. Upon her arrival, Madam Takata went to seek help at a hospital in Akasaka. At the hospital, Madam Takata received even more bad news that she was now suffering from appendicitis and a tumor. With the enormous stress she was under, Madam Takata's weight dropped dramatically. The doctors advised that she undergo surgery immediately. As she was lying in bed that night, Madam Takata heard a voice telling her that surgery was not necessary.

The next day, as Madam Takata was being prepped for her surgery, she heard the voice again. It said the same thing, that surgery was not necessary. Unable to ignore it any longer, Madam Takata asked the surgeon if there was another way that she could be healed without having to undergo the surgery. The doctor told her of a nearby Reiki clinic that was run by Dr. Hayashi. The surgeon's sister was a patient of Dr. Hayashi and had vouched for his abilities. Madam Takata made her way to the clinic where she would spend the next four months undergoing treatments for her various conditions.

By the end of the four months, Madam Takata was completely healed. She decided that she wanted to learn this incredible healing practice that had given her hope once more. She managed to persuade Dr. Hayashi to let her work and train at the clinic for the next twelve months under his mentorship. By the end of the twelve-month period, Madam Takata earned the privilege of advancing to second-degree advanced Reiki practitioner. Madam Takata eventually returned home where she would set up her own Reiki clinic. She spent her days healing patients and teaching Reiki to those who wanted to learn. Dr. Hayashi would later come to visit Madam Takata and invite her to become a Reiki master. Hayashi believed that Madam Takata had gone through many tests and emerged as someone who embodied the Reiki ideals and principles. She was the first woman to be given this honor.

At War with America

At the start of 1940, Japan was close to going to war with America. Dr. Hayashi knew that he would be called upon to fight for the honor of his country. As a man who believed in peace and healing, Dr. Hayashi believed that the most honorable thing to do in this case would be to put his affairs in order. One morning, Madam Takata awoke to a vision of Dr. Hayashi who appeared at the foot of her bed. It was then she realized she needed to make her way to him immediately. Madam Takata met with Dr. Hayashi upon her arrival and Dr. Hayashi explained his decision to get his affairs in order.

They would spend several days planning for the future, and when Dr. Hayashi was satisfied that he had done all he could to safeguard the future of Reiki, he gathered his friends and students together. At the gathering, he declared that Madam Takata would be his successor, and thus become the third grandmaster of Reiki. Dr. Hayashi then dressed in traditional Japanese attire, lay down, and allowed his spirit to leave his body. Some versions of the story believe that Dr. Hayashi committed what is known in Japan as *Seppuku,* otherwise known as *Harakiri*. *Seppuku* or *Harakiri* is the act of stabbing oneself in the heart to bring one's life to an end.

Madam Takata returned home, initiated as the next grandmaster, where she continued her healing and teaching. Madam Takata would go on to train another twenty-two reiki masters before she passed away in December of 1980.

Two other grandmasters were initiated upon Madam Takata's death to carry on her work. One of them was Phyllis Lee Furrumuto, Madam Takata's granddaughter. She was also the founder of the *Reiki Alliance*. The second person was Dr. Barbara Weber. Their partnership would continue for about a year until they decided to go their separate ways for personal reasons. They continued their work on Reiki separately. Dr. Weber founded the AIRA (American International Reiki Association). Today, several associations exist throughout the world, each claiming to possess the only correct way of teaching Reiki. No matter who tries to lay a claim on it though, Reiki ultimately belongs to everyone. It is a gift from the universe and a gift that is meant to be shared by all. This gift is meant to bring people together through the true experience of healing, for we are never happier than when we are healed in mind, body, and soul.

Chapter 3: Becoming a Reiki Practitioner

You're about to embark on a very exciting journey. Reiki healing is unlike any other healing method out there. By learning how to become a Reiki practitioner, you will be one of the few people in this world privy to the knowledge of how the human body can be healed in one of the most natural ways possible.

Steps to Becoming a Practitioner

Before you begin your training, there are a couple of steps that you need to take. The first is to do proper research on the teacher you want to learn from. Find out what their background is, their experience, testimonials, any information you can find to help you decide if this is someone you want to learn from. It is even better if you could meet this teacher in person to get a feel of their energy before your classes commence. This will tell you whether that teacher is someone you can see yourself working with long-term.

Next, figure out what you want to get out of this experience. Identify your goals. What do you want to achieve out of your first few sessions? These goals will help you stay focused and to reflect on whether you're getting the most out of your sessions. Every Reiki session must begin with an intention. You must begin with a purpose in mind, a reason to remind yourself why you are doing this. Think about this intention and have it firmly in your mind before beginning each class. An example of an intention could be wanting to unblock your energy because you've been feeling blocked in a specific area as of late. Reiki is meant to help you balance some of the intense emotions that are going through your mind and body right now, and since this practice is all about being mindful, you must bring to mind your intentions before each session and begin with a clear purpose.

Now, let's begin:

Step 1: Identifying the Signs That You May Have Healing Gifts. Some people have a natural healing ability. One example of this is empaths. Empaths are naturally intuitive individuals who love to help others. They can sense the vibration or the energy from someone else, and this helps them identify when someone might be in need of healing. If you felt like you were drawn to Reiki for a reason, it could be that you have a natural healing tendency and an innate desire to help others. Your ability to heal is your most significant attribute. It is a superpower that you have. Your ability to heal is so unique that in some cases, your presence alone is enough to bring a smile to someone's face when they are feeling down. Empaths also have this uncanny ability to actively listen, which is in itself a tremendous healing power. Active listening is an ability that requires you to be fully present in the conversation. When empaths actively listen, they are giving the other person their undivided attention. These are all skills that come naturally to an empath and are all part of their healing magic.

If you do have any of these gifts or if this is something that you relate to, then learning Reiki is definitely the right choice for you.

Step 2: *Preparing for First Degree Reiki.* If you intend to become a Reiki master one day, there will be two levels of Reiki practice that you need to complete first. These are the First Degree and Second Degree Reiki. As a beginner, you're going to be starting with the First Degree Reiki training to become a practitioner. At this level, you can expect to learn even more about what Reiki is, how it works, and the different types of Reiki systems that exist today. During this first level is where you can expect to receive your first Reiki energy experience with your chosen teacher.

The teacher will start you off with simple exercises to introduce you to the energy force you're trying to connect to. Ideally, this should be done in a quiet and peaceful setting, but if you need on-the-go healing, Reiki can be done anywhere for a quick fix.

Once you have identified the blocked energy area, it's time to focus. Concentrate on the healing process taking place over the energy area. Place your hands over or on the specific area for approximately two to five minutes at a time. If you're attempting to do this on yourself, your hands should experience a warm, tingling sensation as you hold it over your body. Maintain the position until you feel the energy has stopped transitioning out of your body, which is usually when your hands have stopped feeling warm.

During your training, you will be learning the basic techniques about how to use Reiki for stress management, physical, and emotional healing. Your teacher is likely to help you identify where the chakras are located on the body too, since chakras and Reiki are connected as they share that same focus on energy healing. It is best to receive your training in person from a Reiki teacher or master to fully understand what you should be focusing on.

Step 3: Let Go of Your Fear. Stepping out of your comfort zone to try something new is always going to be nerve-wracking. You might not be sure what to expect and you may have no idea whether this was the right choice for you. But with Reiki, you have nothing to fear. Connecting with this universal energy is going to change your life in so many ways, but that can only happen if you're willing to embrace it with an open mind. Fear will always hold you back and fear will keep your mind blocked. When you're blocked (even if you think you are not), you can't allow your mind to fully absorb all the wisdom and the experience that comes with practicing Reiki. Let go of your fear or any hesitations you might have and allow yourself to be fully immersed in the experience.

Step 4: When at Home, Practice Meditating. In between your Reiki sessions, it would be fantastic if you could incorporate some meditation into your routine. Meditation will help to prepare your mind and body to focus. Start small at first by meditating for short periods of time. You could begin with five to ten minutes a day if you're new to it. The reason why you're encouraged to start with small-time blocks like this is that you can do anything for five to ten minutes a day with no resistance, and the time will pass before you even know it. When you see how easy that was and how quickly ten minutes can go by, it keeps you motivated to keep adding onto that. Create small, achievable goals you can accomplish each day, and begin building the habit of making meditation a part of your daily life. This will help you better prepare for the Second Degree Reiki training, which focuses on healing on a spiritual level. First Degree Reiki training focuses on healing the physical body.

Step 5: Create A Comfortable Space at Home to Practice. Creating a space within your home that you actually look forward to spending some time in, is an essential part of establishing a consistent Reiki practice. This comfortable space should be designed solely for your Reiki practice sessions, or healing sessions if you have people in your home you would like to practice this on. This space could be anything you want it to be, and you're free to make it as comfortable as you need. Fill it with pillows, inspiring pictures, healing crystals for energy and balance, incense, scented candles, anything that helps to soothe your soul.

Common Questions About Becoming a Practitioner

When starting anything new, it is common to have a lot of questions. If you're reading this, you likely have a few, and want to know as much as possible about what it takes to become a Reiki practitioner. Let's answer some of these questions right now:

- **What Do You Do As A Practitioner** - As a Reiki practitioner, you're going to be doing a lot of healing using your hands. You will be channeling the universal life force energy *into* the person you are trying to heal. If you're attempting to heal yourself, you would be channeling the life force energy back into your own body. As you're channeling this energy, you're going to help your patients feel relaxed and comfortable, diminishing any stress they might have felt when they came to you. By helping the energy move around the person's body (or your own body), you're helping to correct the energy flow that might have been blocked for certain reasons.

- **What Benefits Do We Get from Healing This Way?** There are a lot of reasons why you should be using Reiki as a method of healing. The first benefit is that it is all-natural, and anytime something is natural, it is always good for the body. You're working with what the body already has instead of putting something in your body that maybe shouldn't be there. Healing your energy from within forces you to stop, slow down, and take a moment to be mindful. Aside from healing yourself physically, Reiki also allows you to heal mentally and spiritually.

- **Can I Learn Reiki?** - Yes, you can. You don't have to have spent a lifetime in search of spiritual awakening or have any special skills. If you want to learn, that willingness and eagerness to learn are all that you need to get started. Anyone can connect to this powerful and simple system of healing, even young children. It is safe enough for anyone to learn. You don't need to make any special preparations before you begin taking classes either. Your Reiki classes will focus on learning how to react to the subtle energies of the body.

- **Am I Going to Be Certified as A Practitioner?** - When you undergo training with a Reiki master, you should receive a certificate at the end of your training program. The certificate should state that you have successfully completed your Reiki training. The certificate will allow you to use the title of Reiki Practitioner when you're carrying out healing sessions on others. Now, a certificate is not the same as a license. You will *not* be a licensed practitioner with just a certificate. If you intend to be a professional practitioner, it is a good idea to check with your local council to see if you require any sort of permit to do so.

- **Is It Okay If I Don't Want to Open A Practice?** Yes, of course it is. Many people learn Reiki purely for their own benefit.

Like everything else, Reiki is a practice that is going to take time to master. Don't be discouraged if you don't see or feel anything from your very first session, that is normal.

Your Reiki capabilities are like a muscle, the more you work on them, the better and stronger they are going to become. Eventually, Reiki healing will become second nature if you dedicate yourself to it.

Chapter 4: Reiki's Healing Magic

The idea that anyone can learn to practice Reiki without having to go through years of study or practice is wonderful. This means that you don't have to wait for years before you can begin experiencing the healing magic of Reiki. All you need is the right Reiki Master to teach you the basics and pass that energy on to you. What the Reiki Master will be giving you is a gift known as a *Reiki Attunement*.

What Is Reiki Attunement?

Reiki Attunement is a very powerful, spiritual experience. Through the process, the Reiki Master will open the *crown, heart, and palm* chakra points in your body. The *crown chakra* sits right at the top of your head. Right at the crown, and since the crown of the head is the highest point of the human body, the crown chakra represents your beliefs and your awareness of higher powers. Those who struggle to maintain a balance of the crown chakra find themselves dealing with boredom, depression, confusion at times, and limiting beliefs that hold them back from reaching their full potential. The *heart chakra* is right at the center of your chest. Matters of the heart are almost always linked back to love.

The *heart chakra* has a lot to do with how much love you give and take, and to find balance within this chakra means there must be equal parts give and take. You can't give too much without receiving in return, and you can't take too much either without giving anything back. When your *heart chakra* is not balanced, you are likely to experience a lot of heart-related troubles. Chest pains, difficulty breathing deeply, heart attacks, rapid heart rate, or heart palpitations are just some of the problems you can expect. But find balance in your *heart chakra* and your life will be filled with all the love and support you could ever want. The *palm chakras* are located in the middle of each palm of your hand. This makes the hands extremely useful for channeling energy and healing, which is why Reiki relies heavily on the use of your hands to initiate the healing process. Your *palm chakras* are the focal points of your hand meridians. Our hands are meant to heal, give, and receive energy.

There is a reason the Reiki master will focus on opening these three specific chakras to initiate the attunement process. The opening of these chakras will create a very special connection between you (the student) and the Reiki source. This energy transfer process can be done from one person to the next, which is part of the reason why Reiki is such a magical ability. There is no other healing technique in the world that is like it. The energy that is passed onto you will be different from what another student might need. Every student is different, and your experience might not be the same as someone else's.

When you restore your chakras and your energy to their relaxed, healthy, and natural flow, you're balancing them. Since it is nearly impossible to remain relaxed or calm all the time in our daily lives, our chakras get put out of balance from the anxious emotions, thoughts, and feelings that we experience. This overload of emotions disrupts your chakras and thus, your energy becomes blocked.

Once you have achieved attunement, you will finally have the ability to heal others through Reiki. Once the energy has been passed to you from the Reiki Master, it will never leave you. This knowledge, this wisdom, will remain with you for the rest of your life. Once your eyes have been opened to the energy and life force that surrounds every living being in this world, there is no going back.

Since there are multiple levels of Reiki, you will need an attunement each time you move up the ladder. While you only need one attunement for each level, there is nothing wrong with having more than one attunement either. In fact, it could be beneficial to have more these attunements regularly to ensure that your chakras are staying balanced and unblocked.

Reiki's Healing Magic - Level One

In level one, you will learn to heal others through your hands. While level one is mainly meant to help you heal yourself, the ability to heal through your hands means you will be able to heal others too. This attunement can be achieved at any age, and it only takes about a day for you to receive this gift. The basic Reiki learned at this level should be practiced regularly, even better if you can carve out some time daily to practice what you have learned.

Reiki's Healing Magic - Level Two

Level two's healing magic is at least *four times* more powerful than what you would have learned in level one. Once you have advanced to level two, you will have the ability to provide distance healing for others. You should practice level one for at least three months before you attempt to advance to level two. This ensures that your body is cleansed appropriately, preparing you to receive the attunement.

Reiki's Healing Magic - Level Three

This is the Master healer's level. This is at least *ten times* more powerful than the second level. Once you have advanced to this level, you are able to send healing powers to anyone through your thoughts. That's right, just your thoughts and nothing else. That is how remarkable this level of healing is. Ideally, you should have been practicing the other levels of Reiki for at least a year or two before you attempt to achieve attunement at this level.

By this stage, you would have also reached the *Teacher-Master* level, and you will be able to attune others. The final stage of this level is where you achieve the Reiki *Grandmaster* level. Once you have reached the final level, you have the ability to attune others at any level. Ascending to the level of *Grandmaster* is not something you can ask for. It is something that must be offered to you by the teacher if they see the potential within you.

As with everything else, Reiki treatments only get better with practice. It is important to make your Reiki training a daily practice to advance and improve as quickly as possible. Within your home, create a space where you can carry out this practice in a calm, focused, relaxed manner. Having this space in your home that you actually look forward to spending some time in is an essential part of establishing a consistent meditation practice. This comfortable space should be designed solely for your meditation sessions. This space could be anything you want it to be, and you're free to make it as comfortable as you need. Fill it with pillows, inspiring pictures, healing crystals for energy and balance, incense, scented candles, anything that helps to soothe your soul. You need to feel happy and positive within this space so your chakras can undergo the healing that they need to restore balance. When you have a space to look forward to using because you love the warmth, calm, and feeling of peace that envelopes you each time you're there, you'll be eager to practice your Reiki every day just to feel good.

Reiki Healing Tips

Whether you intend to use Reiki to heal yourself or others, there are several things to keep in mind. It is going to take at least three weeks to fully feel the effects of your newfound abilities. During these three weeks, your body is going to cleanse and heal itself naturally to get rid of negative energy. To help the process along, a good tip would be to make sure you're getting enough sleep and are drinking plenty of water.

To fine-tune your abilities, you need to be practicing your chakra abilities every day. In your daily routine, you might encounter a lot of moments that infuse you with negative emotions and tasks that drain you of energy. By the time you're ready for bed at night, you've probably picked up a lot of negative energy along the way and you're now running low and feeling tired. Practicing Reiki every day is a way to replenish this lost energy while cleansing your body, mind, and soul at the same time. It is okay to practice a few times a week also, but avoid going too long without practicing your skills. Negative energy is something we are exposed to daily, and if you don't make it a habit to regularly cleanse, your chakras can quickly become blocked and you'll struggle to achieve the healing you need. Re-attunement may be necessary if too much time passes between your Reiki sessions.

Another tip to remember is to work around your schedule and to be flexible with your practice times. Some days, you might have only five minutes to squeeze in for a quick practice session. Other times, you might have fifteen or twenty minutes to spare. It is okay to work around your schedule. The important thing is that you *don't neglect* your practice.

When you're practicing Reiki, keep the following tips in mind:

- **Do It with Your Eyes Open** - This applies when you're trying to heal someone else. Stay focused and stay present. You are there to help someone, and you can't pay attention on the other person if your eyes are closed.

- **Be Mindful** - Pay attention during the healing process. Focus on the healing and nothing else. Be mindful of every step, gesture, feeling, emotion, and energy that you feel. If you're not present and being mindful, it is hard to immerse yourself in the experience.

- **Wear Something Comfortable -** You're not going to be able to get anything done when you're fidgeting all over the place because you're uncomfortable. Avoid any clothing that is too restrictive, what you wear should allow you to breathe and move comfortably when you need to.

- **Have an Open Mind and A Peaceful Heart -** Reiki is not a competition to see who can be the best or who can master the art of Reiki the fastest. Everyone is different, and we all learn at our own pace. Some practitioners might be able to get the hang of it faster than others, and if they happen to grasp the concept of Reiki faster than you do, don't be discouraged. Just come to each session with an open mind and a peaceful heart and you'll do fine.

- **Begin Each Session by Setting Positive Intentions -** Whether you're practicing alone at home or are healing someone else, begin each session with a positive intention. For example, if you come to each session with an intention to thrive and enjoy every moment of it, the experience you get from each session is going to be far more beneficial than if you came with no intention at all.

- **Clear Your Mind Before You Begin** - A common mistake that gets made is when people don't take the time to clear their thoughts or calm themselves down before beginning a meditation session. It's fine if you're doing your sessions in the morning after waking up because your mind is not yet boggled by everything that has gone on during the day. But if you're doing your sessions at the end of the day, calming your mind is an essential task that you need to make a part of your practice. Everything that we see, hear and experience throughout the day will have an impact on us, whether we realize it or not, and if we attempt to enter a healing state with our minds clouded by other thoughts, it's going to make it harder for you to concentrate. Take a few moments before you begin to just walk around, relax, loosen up, and clear your mind.

- **Avoid Selfishness** - Reiki is a selfless practice. If you choose to practice Reiki in a way that purely for personal gain with no intention to help anyone, you're going to have a hard time connecting with what the true spirit of Reiki is all about. This is why it is important to set a positive intention. If you come to your Reiki session with nothing but good intentions, there will be no room for selfishness.

- **Create the Right Environment** - The right environment is either going to make or break the success of your session. Creating the perfect environment is the first part of a successful deep Reiki session. The second part, of course, is to ensure that the room has the right kind of ambiance. Specifically, the lighting. Candles work very well in this instance. Low lighting can relax the mind a lot quicker than fluorescent or bright lights will, so consider filling your room with natural or soft lighting.

Chapter 5: Reiki Self-Help – Can It Be Done?

What if you had a way to increase your self-awareness? A way to heal yourself of any issues and feel better about the challenges or obstacles you may be facing in your life? What if you had a way to feel more energized, and the ability to navigate your way through life successfully no matter what came your way without feeling drained, lethargic, or at a loss? Reiki can help you to achieve all of the above!

What to Expect With Self-Healing

Self-healing in Reiki uses different hand positions than the ones you would use to heal others. During your training, your Reiki master should guide you and show you how your hands should be positioned when you're healing yourself. For the best results, you should aim to practice self-healing as consistently as you can. Practicing for an hour a day is more than good enough, but avoid spending the entire time focusing on the problem area alone. Reiki works as a system. Energy is always on the move, constantly changing even when you think nothing is happening.

For the next few days, observe yourself as you go throughout your day. What you will notice is that certain situations, places, and people, can deplete our energy levels. For example, when we feel present, and when we're mindful, our energy is rooted and strong. When we feel repulsion or attraction, we feel energetically charged. That's one example of the way that your energy moves about. When we unblock our energy centers, our minds become open, flexible and our breathing becomes rhythmic. It feels as though your body is opening, creating more space within itself. When your mind is opened completely, you enable yourself to achieve a healthy balance between contraction and expansion, activation, and receptivity. Our energy is never a stagnant thing because our emotions are not stagnant. Your energy reflects your current health and state of mind, and if your emotions change, your energy changes along with it. Everyone goes through a range of emotions daily, and this means your energy is also going to shift and change throughout the day, depending on how you feel.

The Benefits of Self-Healing

When you have the ability to heal yourself, you no longer have to rely on anyone else whenever you're in need. Reiki has the ability to heal allergies, premenstrual symptoms, thyroid issues, and so much more. Although your conditions might not improve overnight, especially if you have been dealing with them for years, a consistent practice should still yield a noticeable improvement in your health. Once your health has improved, Reiki can then be used as preventative maintenance. Consistent practice makes your cells feel energized, and it will be harder for ailments to set in.

Self-healing Reiki is a great tool to keep you from burning out. Once you experience the benefits of self-healing firsthand, you will be inspired to help others because you know what a difference it can make. Self-care has gained a lot of attention in recent years as we start to recognize the importance of slowing down every now and then to find balance in our lives. Looking after yourself is *not* a selfish activity, and it is a good thing we are slowly moving away from that kind of thinking. You cannot fill someone else's cup if your own cup is empty.

What to Do Before You Begin

Before you begin your self-healing sessions, observe your energy when you are moving. Move your body, move different parts at a time, and observe how you feel when you move. Do you notice any kinds of thoughts or feelings that arise? Are there certain parts of your body that are energized when you move? Did a particular movement stir something up inside you? Do you feel like you need to contain your energy? This will help you figure which areas of your body need more healing than others.

During the self-healing process, you will learn how to sense your energy. Sensing energy is not going to be an easy task right away. Sensing energy is probably something you've never attempted until now, but it is a method you need to learn before you can start learning how to manipulate and move energy. Close your eyes and start by visualizing your body. This time, instead of focusing on your energy, you're going to be focusing on the veins in your body instead. Visualize the veins you see clearly in your mind's eye, but instead of picturing them red with blood, picture them carrying energy around your body. See the energy circling through your body touching each and every nerve. Next, try sensing the vibrations that you feel while this energy circulates throughout your body through the veins. Focus on a specific body part, such as your arm, and tell the energy in your body to course specifically to that area. Once you are done moving the energy around your body, allow the energy to flow naturally again throughout your body. As you perform these exercises, it is important not to feel disappointed if you don't experience any sensations or feelings the first time you do it.

It might help if you sit in silence for several moments before you attempt your healing sessions. Find a space where you can be in absolute quiet, and just sit in silence, that's all you need to do. Don't think about anything in particular. Sit in silence and wait until your mind settles down on its own. If you can, meditate for several minutes to calm your mind.

How to Perform the Self-Healing Process

To begin the self-healing process, you should place your hands on the following areas of your body, and in the following order:

- **Hand Position 1 - On the Crown of Your Head.** Place one palm at the front of your forehead and the other at the back. Keep your hands in that position while breathing in and out deeply. Tune in to the breath as you inhale and exhale. Inhale the positive energy and exhale any negativity or stress that you feel. Close your eyes and visualize the stress leaving your body. Let this position promote healing of your mind and let the sense of relaxation travel throughout your entire being from your head to your toes.

- **Hand Position 2 - On Your Face.** Continue your deep breathing in this position. Focus on the breath as you inhale and exhale. You can cup your hands over your eyes or place them on any area of your face where you're feeling pain, discomfort, or stress. As you keep your hands in this position, allow the warmth from your palms to relax the skin all-around your face. Feel your muscles relax with each exhale.

- **Hand Position 3 - On Your Throat**. Keep your steady breathing rhythm as you transition to this position. Keep going as long as you need until you feel the muscles around your neck and shoulders relax completely.

- **Hand Position 4 - At the Back of Your Head**. As you make the transition from your throat to the back of your head, don't lose the steady rhythm you have been keeping with your breath. Resting your hands at the back of your head will help to soothe any of the headaches and stress-related tension you feel. We don't realize how much weight we carry at the back of our head and the shoulders from all the stress that we feel, and it is important to take the time to heal this part of your body. It should feel like a huge weight has been lifted off your shoulders once you've completed this position. Another thing you can do while in this position is slowly move your hands down to your shoulders and gently massage the area for a few minutes. Not only does a massage feel good physically, it's also great for balancing your energy and your chakras. Massaging the area gently while breathing deeply encourages the flow of energy to this region and gets the blood circulating through the muscles.

- **Hand Position 5 - On the Upper Chest.** The healing in this position will open your chest muscles, allowing the heart to pump blood freely through your body. Bring your hands to the heart and rub your hands together to create warmth. Next, place one hand on your upper chest and one hand resting below that.

- **Hand Position 6 - On the Lower Ribs**. Your hands should be placed just below your breast line. Close your eyes and focus your energy on this area, channeling your healing powers to your solar plexus. Maintain this position for at least two minutes to allow the healing process to take place.

- **Hand Position 7 - On the Belly Button**. This is another area where you can gently give yourself a massage to stimulate the blood flow and the flow of energy. Massage your abdominal area in a clockwise motion, focusing around the navel. The circulation should also stimulate and open your heart center. Leave your hands in this position as your focus on your breath.

- **Hand Position 8 - On the Lower Abdomen**. From the belly button position, begin to transition your hands down to your lower abdomen. Keep breathing and massaging this area if you feel you need to. If you don't, then simply allow your hands to be placed comfortably on this area and feel the warmth and energy from your palms work their magic.

As you move through the different areas of your body, place your hands on each section anywhere from thirty seconds to one minute. Let the warmth from your hands disperse any pain that you feel. The whole idea of focusing on your breath as you work your way through the various hand positions is to help you stay focused on the present. When your mind has something to focus on (like your breath), you're less likely to get distracted.

Is There a Perfect Time to Begin the Self-Healing Process?

There is no "perfect" for you to practice self-healing, but you do need to be in the right frame of mind before you begin. Avoid self-healing when you're feeling bored, restless, lethargic, or disinterested because that's a sure-fire way to quickly lose interest, and not be able to follow through with the session that you started. You won't be thinking clearly, and you'll subconsciously be resisting it because it's not where you want to be right now. If you're not in the right frame of mind, don't do it, and instead, wait until you're ready.

Many people do find it helpful to practice their Reiki sessions first thing in the morning, but it is entirely up to you and what suits you best. It can be any time of the day, and if you find evening works best for you, go with that. This process should be entirely yours; copying what someone else is trying to do is not going to yield the same benefit. It is going to take some trial and error when you first begin your practice to figure out the best time of the day for you, but you will get there eventually.

You might also like to try some soothing music in the background. Soothing music during a healing session can do wonders to engulf you with a sense of calm and tranquility, and you will find it much easier to sink into a deep, focused state with the help of the right kind of music.

Final Tips

It is okay to use a timer during your practice sessions as long as the timer emits a pleasant, soothing, calming noise. Avoid any timers that are harsh and loud, as this will disrupt the sense of tranquility you were building during your sessions. As a Reiki healer, it is important to cultivate your empathetic abilities too. Empathy will help you anticipate the needs of others because you'll be able to recognize the emotions and the needs that they are displaying.

It is also a good idea to keep a journal of your Reiki practice sessions to make a note of any insights, ideas, or inspirations that you have. Also remember, there is no wrong way to place your hands on your body. As long as you set an intention, stay focused, and practice as best you can, that is more than good enough to start with. You don't have to be perfect before you begin practicing your healing. All you need is to be confident enough in your abilities and have a genuine desire to help others.

Chapter 6: Using Reiki on Others

Once you have learned the healing wisdom of Reiki, you never have to sit back and feel helpless again as you watch a loved one struggle. You will now have what you need to help them in the best way that you know. The best part is, this type of healing is so natural that there is no possible way you could make the situation any worse. All you need is a pure heart and a strong desire to heal, and the healing magic of Reiki will take care of the rest.

What You Need Before You Begin

The beauty of Reiki is how easy it is to perform. Before you begin, all you need is awareness and concentration. Yes, it really is as simple as performing these healing techniques on yourself. Just like you did when you practiced these healing techniques on yourself, you want to keep an open mind. Remember, Reiki is a gift, and it is a power that is bigger than any of us. Any kind of resistance to the practice is going to make it very difficult to reap the full benefits.

It is equally important to remember that we should never judge anyone who comes to us for healing. Their problems and personal troubles are their burdens to carry, and it is not for you to judge them or share your opinions about what they come to you for treatment of. Your job is to focus on the healing, which is what they came to you for. Give them the help that they seek, and they will leave your session feeling happy. Avoid judgment because it will act as a mental block *for you* and prevent you from being open to receiving the healing energy you need from the universe.

How to Heal Others

To begin, you need to activate your chakras and energy by rubbing the palms of your hands together. Doing so will help you connect to the Reiki energy, and you can then begin the transference process. The first step of the process is for you to receive your energy. When rubbing the palms of your hands together, close your eyes, and connect with your breath. Imagine yourself filling up with positive energy that you are preparing to transfer to the person in front of you. Let this feeling envelop you completely as you calm your mind. Visualize yourself as a healing vessel, and then you're ready to move on to the healing:

- **First Position: Healing the Crown Chakra** - Once you've activated your energy, you want to start at the person's crown chakra. Place your hands so your thumbs meet, forming the diamond position. Now, slowly place it at the crown of the person's head and concentrate on feeling their energy. You don't need to touch the person's head, but rather hover an inch or two above the crown. As the highest point on the human body, the crown of the head represents your beliefs and your awareness of higher powers. Those who struggle to maintain a balance of the seventh chakra find themselves dealing with boredom, depression, confusion at times, and limiting beliefs that hold them back from reaching their full potential. By healing this point of their body, you will help them feel at peace. You will help them feel like they are one with the universe. You are helping them feel connected to themselves and the people around them, and the clarity they will experience will make them feel rejuvenated once more.

- **Second Position: Above the Eyes -** This energy point is called the *Third-Eye Chakra*. Again, all you will need to do is hover your hands an inch or two above the person's eyes. Their eyes should be closed while you begin the healing process. The area that you are going to focus on healing is right between the eyes, and re-energizing this area helps with mental clarity.

- **Third Position: Hands Behind the Head** - Gently place your hands on either side of the person's head and slowly roll their head from side to side, helping to relax this area. The third eye chakra, linked to the pituitary gland or autonomic nervous system, is where your spiritual energy and higher intuition reside. Where the third eye chakra resides is also where the pineal and pituitary glands are, governing the area around our eyes, brain, and skull. This chakra affects the way our nervous system and senses feel. Your fingertips should be positioned at the base of the skull. Your two little fingers should be touching each other as you do this. This will allow you to cup the back of the person's head in the right manner. This healing position is good for curing any stress, tension, and headaches, especially if the person is prone to a lot of overthinking. It is also a great healing practice for balancing blood pressure.

- **Fourth Position: Hands Over the Ears** - Gently place your hands over the person's ears. Your fingertips should be rested against their jaw when doing this correctly. From here, you can transition your hands back and forth between the ears and move inward towards the eyebrows. While at the eyebrows, your fingertips should have a firm touch on the eyebrows. This will help heal their sinuses. You can also choose to perform this healing by placing your fingertips on the cheekbones. It should be the area where the cheekbones meet the bridge of the nose. This is another healing method that is good for those with a tendency to overthink.

- **Fifth Position: Behind the Shoulders** - Place your hands underneath the person's body, with your thumbs directly around the shoulder blades area. The rest of your hands should be able to cup the person over the shoulders, forming a C-shape with your hands. This will allow you to transition to the throat chakra as you begin transferring the energy around this area, helping it move along. An imbalance or blockage of the throat energy leaves you with difficulty speaking up when you need to, especially when you have to stand up for yourself. Stiff shoulders, sore throats, and a stiff neck will follow you around until you find a way to balance out this energy again.

- **Sixth Position: The Chest** - From the throat area, your hands will now begin to transition to the chest, and then move all the way down the torso. Your hands should be hovering a few inches right above these areas. The chest area is also where the heart chakra resides, and it has a lot to do with how much love you give and take.

As for the healing of the solar plexus, this is really important for young children and teenagers in particular who might be undergoing a lot of stress in their life. A lot of the worries and tension that might be held in the stomach area will be released once this energy center has been unblocked. Chakra practitioners believe that the solar plexus region connects to your self-esteem and vitality for life. This not only affects you but the people around you too. The company that you keep, the food you eat, and your self-esteem connect to this area of your body. Digestive and abdominal issues are among the physical symptoms associated with the solar plexus. Heal this region and the person should notice a very significant difference in their vitality and outlook on life.

- **Seventh Position: Below the Navel -** This area is also known to chakra practitioners as the *Sacral Chakra* region. This area is where the reproductive organs are located. Healing this region works wonders on those struggling with PMS, mood swings, and other emotional imbalances in their life. You can rotate your hands to position them on either side of a person's hips too when you do this, transferring the energy all throughout this region.

- **Eighth Position: Knees, Calves, and Ankles** - The transition should be in a smooth flow from the knees all the way down to your ankles. You don't have to rush this process, take your time hovering over each area, focusing on feeling the energy before you move onto the next. The ankles and the feet should be the final step of the healing process in your Reiki practice. This position heals what chakra practitioners call the *Root Chakra*. When this area is blocked, it prevents you from feeling grounded and centered. The easiest way to tell that there's a problem is when you're too caught up in your own thoughts. When the energy in this area is blocked, you may resort to behaviors you wouldn't normally do in a misguided attempt to feel grounded. Feeling sluggish, mentally feeling like you're stuck and unable to move forward, chronic stress, persistent financial troubles, feelings of abandonment and isolation, anger, frustration or hatred towards yourself and others, and constantly feeling like nothing you do is ever good enough are all related to a blocked Root Chakra. Physical symptoms include stiffness and pain in your legs and feet, no sense of physical stability, sciatica, constipation, too much flexibility around the hamstring area, rectal/anal problems, varicose veins, diarrhea, impotence, problems with groin, water retention, calves, and ankles. The ankles are also a good place to perform healing since your feet are considered your "roots." Place your hands underneath their ankles first when you're performing this healing, and then transition to the top of the ankles. Move your way along the foot slowly until you finally place your thumb behind the big toe of each foot while the rest of your hands grips the feet.

There you have it, some of the basic hand positions you need to know if you want to use your Reiki gifts to heal others.

Final Key Point to Remember

Your healing is only going to be as effective as you are. You *must* heal yourself before you can heal someone else. If you try to heal another but you harbor a belief in illnesses yourself, or you have a lot of suffering, stress, and anxieties within you, your healing sessions are not going to be as powerful as you hoped. If you lack clarity, it is not possible to transfer love and healing to someone else.

To be the best kind of healer you can be, you need to be convinced that illness and physical pain have no power over you. You must believe that you are stronger than anything that can threaten to bring you down. To be able to heal yourself and others, you must affirm that you are no longer a victim of any kind of illness or physical pain.

Conclusion

Thank you for making it through to the end of *Reiki*, let's hope it was informative and able to provide you with all the tools you need to achieve your goals whatever they may be.

If you're interested in learning more about Reiki and becoming a practitioner yourself, search for a Reiki Master in your local area!

Remember, Reiki has a lot of benefits, however it should not be used to entirely replace modern medicine, particularly for serious medical conditions. Fortunately, it can be used in conjunction with regular treatments, oftentimes with great effect!

Once again, thank you for choosing the book. I wish you the best of luck on your Reiki journey!

www.ingramcontent.com/pod-product-compliance
Lightning Source LLC
LaVergne TN
LVHW021736060526
838200LV00052B/3317